The voyage of Zeenat

Main Casts:

1. <u>Zeenat / Ankita</u>: lead character

2. <u>Sundar Iyer</u>: Brahman from Palakkad, Kerala, father of Zeenat. Works in an NGO and travels across India.

3. <u>Zeba</u>: Mother of Zeenat, from Hunza Valley Pakistan. She works as dancer / standee girl in a Mujra Bar in Dubai

4. <u>Dadda</u>: Father of Sundar Iyer. A very strict guy lives in Palakkad.

5. <u>Shazia / Badi Apa</u> – works as dancer in Dubai Mujra club. Later become women trafficking mafia and operates out of Aligarh, UP. She raises Zeenat.

6. <u>Shahjad Mia</u>: mentor of Zeenat and helps her study. He is Maulwi and lives in Aligarh.

7. <u>Gaurav</u>: Zeenat's friend and potential love interest. Childhood in Aligarh, then Mumbai.

8. <u>Rahman</u> – Dance bar manager in Mumbai. Zeenat stays in his house and studies.

9. <u>Cheera Bhai</u> – left hand of Badi Apa and manages her nexus of women trafficking in Dubai and meets the demand of Sheikh

10. <u>Adilah</u> – A lady in Dubai who helps Zeenat see her mother birth place in Pakistan.

11. <u>Viral</u> – politician in India

12. <u>Suja Logo</u> – drug mafia who runs a prostitution racket.

Sub cast

1. Waiter – In Dubai Mujra bar

2. Gaurav Mother – housewife

3. Gaurav Father – floor manager in Lock Company

4. Shabnam – Badi apa's manager, lives in Aligarh.

5. Roshani – Zeenat's friend in dance bar

6. Bouncer – in Mumbai dance bar in white dress.

7. Sanu – Gaurav's cameraman

8. Zunaid – Adilah's driver who has crush on Adilah.

Chapter 1: Sundar family and overseas assignment

Sundar Iyer belongs to a Tamil Brahman family from Palakkad District of Kerala. Palakkad district is located at the border of Kerala and Tamilnadu and known for the extremely intelligent and learned people. The locale of Palakkad is very much dominated by Brahmins who migrated from Tanjjavur district of Tamilnadu. Palakkad is known for its cultural richness in terms of the heritage and literacy. Sundar Iyer was fair, handsome guy with 5 feet 11 inch height.

Sundar Iyer's father, whom he calls Dadda believes in traditional values and never ready to compromise when it comes to culture and character. Dadda is a disciplined, highly strict and tried his level best to inculcate Hindu customs to Sundar Iyer. Sundar Iyer on the other hand behaves in front of his father but believes in living a free life. Sundar Iyer drinks, smokes and enjoys hanging out with his close friends but still vegetarian. His limit of drinking was 2 glass of beer. After that he needed Curd Rice and feels better. His friend used to laugh at him that curd or any sour food cuts the effect of alcohol. Despite all this Sundar never changed.

Sundar Iyer completed his masters in literature and got a job in an international NGO who supports the human affairs and helps in promoting education as part of life. During his job, he also gets an opportunity to attend conferences, learn and do research but he is not supposed to indulge in any kind of discussion publically as sometime he has to do a surprise visit to some universities to know the reality and the fact of the ground. This time he got an assignment to travel to Dubai for three months, he shares this with Dadda only and takes his blessings.

Chapter 2: Sundar in Dubai and meets Zeba

This is late 90's when the outflow of Indian going outside India was a prestigious thing, at the same time technology has just evolved but keeping Mobile phone and desktop computer was a luxury. We are talking about the year 1997; Sundar was in Dubai for 3 months. He was putting up in Bur Dubai area. During that time Dubai was going through transition and it was converting into a total cosmopolitan city. Same time Mujra Bar has started in Dubai predominantly run by Indian or Pakistanis. The girls were coming from India, Bangladesh, Sri Lanka and Pakistan and supposed to dance or do standee job. Hindi songs were quite popular in Dubai and Khan Trio has emerged as the biggest connecting link for the people in Pakistan and Bangladesh. Sundar used to speak decent Hindi but his dialect was Malayalam.

It's Thursday which is last working day of the week, at 9PM Sundar is relaxing in his room and reading a book named "The Moor's Last Sigh" by Salman Rushdie, suddenly he gets up to stretch his body and sees outside window, then he wears jeans, shirt and shoes and decided to take a walk and also explore a place to have couple of drinks. He came out from his apartment and took Taxi and asked him to take a place where he can drink, Taxi dropped him to a nice hotel and indicates him upstairs. Sundar Iyer entered the hotel and asks a gatekeeper about the pub, he indicates him to go to the 7th Floor. When he reaches seventh floor, he sees two very heavy built guys wearing full black suit and standing outside the gate. Both of them shook hand with Sundar and let him in.

Sundar to his surprise reaches a Mujra Bar, where at least 20 pretty girls are standing and one dancing to the tune of "Pardesi – Pardesi jana nahin". Other girls see him and smiles, he was bit uncomfortable but did not feel right to go back as he knew getting beer in Dubai is not easy. Same time a waiter came and shook hands with him.

Since it was first time Sundar reached that bar he got good welcome by many guys shaking hands with him. They called a girl to dance in front of Sundar and ran a special song for him "Aye ho meri zindagi me tum Bahar banke". There was nothing great in that song for Sundar (also he being south Indian) but he liked the dance. He settles down and having beer, then he sees a girl standing in the corner and watching her palms and bit unrest and uncomfortable. Her name is Zeba.

Vertically at the roof, there was a small bulb and that light was coming directly on Zeba's face and then reaching to her palms which she was busy looking at. In that light, she was looking stunning and Sundar gets completely mesmerized. Sundar could not take his eyes out from her face. She after few seconds lifts her head up and start watching around then suddenly sees Sundar staring her with open mouth. Sundar was looking very cute and Zeba couldn't stop her laugh. Sundar then realized that he is staring at her like an idiot.

It was first time when Sundar saw that people are throwing money on girls like crazy, he wasn't comfortable with that and couldn't afford too. He called waiter and asked him about the process of money throwing. Waiter explains him various rates such as to call any girl in front of you, you may give 10 Dirham, for song choice 100 Dirham, for girl dancing on your favorite song is 500 Dirham. Then waiter indicates all the best to him and said "Please Enjoy Sir" which he didn't like and murmured "What enjoy by throwing money like idiot".

Sundar kept looking at Zeba as he had never seen such a pretty girl in his whole life so he kept looking at her until she sees him staring. This drama of Sundar and Zeba continues and when there are eye contact both smiles. There was girl in the same Pub named Shazia looks at both of them and smiles. Waiter also noticed it and smiled. After two beers Sundar is done and needed curd rice, he decides to leave the place and settles the bill. After bill was settled, waiter asked him for tip, he leaves chiller. Waiter then says him "sir how about that girl you were staring at?" Sundar gets pissed off and asks Waiter "Do I need to pay money for staring any Girl?" Waiter says "No Sir, not necessary, but that way you may see her closely. It helps." Sundar then takes out 10 Dirham note and gives that in waiter to give it that girl, waiter tells him "Hold a second sir" and calls Zeba. Zeba comes in front of Sundar and Sundar in anxiety stands up and offers right hand for hand shake. Zeba blushes and shakes hand with Sundar too. Waiter says "Sir, please also offer token". Sundar gives her

10 Dirham which Zeba accepts nicely and then he speedily came out of the Pub and out of the hotel. After coming out of the hotel, he takes a long breath and sits in taxi to go back home.

In his apartment, Sundar sees his palm in the dim light and smiles and very happy and remembers Zeba with the background sound of "Aye ho meri Zindagi me tum bahar ban ke".

Now it has become routine and every Thursday Sundar will go to that bar, sit and drink 2 glass of beer, keep looking at Zeba. Both smile at each other, Shazia and Waiter will see both of them smile. Waiter will come to Sundar and ask irritating questions "Sir, why did you not come on the other day of the week" Sundar replies "I have other work too than sitting here" waiter responds "Then why did you come today Sir?" Sundar angrily sees him and then waiter says "OK Sir, Enjoy." After two beers, Sundar will call Zeba shakes hand and give 10 dirham.

Sundar and waiter conversation also becomes exciting. Some other day waiter will say like "Sir, your Shirt is very nice." Sundar says "Thank you". Waiter further says "Green color suits on you Sir." Sundar then responds "Green is my favorite color". Waiter will finally irritate him "Great sir, but why you wear same jeans every day?" Sundar will look at him angrily and then finally waiter will say "Ok Sir, Enjoy".

Well, Zeba is from a place called Hunja valley in Pakistan. Hunja valley is situated in North West of Pakistan and known for the natural beauty and serene environment. It is also famous for the most beautiful women and their longevity, which is quite obvious living in that place. Zeba came in Dubai one week before Sundar and started going in Pub every day. Initially it was quite boring and frustrating for her but after meeting Sundar and when eye game started, she waits for Thursday and Sundar too. But interestingly, they don't know each other's name. They never bothered to ask that and busy playing eye game. In fact same waiter asked him one day "Sir, it seems you come to see her only". Sundar says "Do you have any problem with that?" Waiter replies "No Sir, but do you know her name?" Sundar responds "How does it matter?" Waiter "You are right sir, it doesn't matter" Sundar then asks "By the way what is her name?" Waiter says "How does it matter Sir" Sundar sees him angrily and then waiter says "Ok Sir, Enjoy".

This went for 5 week; Thursday night was like date for Sundar and Zeba. For Zeba, Sundar was very special person in her life to an extent she will not spend 10 Dirham and keep it in a beautiful box where she used to keep all kind of bills for food, bus, flight, electricity and whatsoever she gets.

Shazia who stays with Zeba in a same room will tease Zeba for Sundar and their eye game. Shazia also told Zeba that she should run away with Sundar before it is too late for her.

Shazia is from Aligarh, India and very cunning girl. She knows her business well; she understands the game to manage her clients and the way to addict them to come to club. This way she also makes money by connecting his clients to other girls in the club and makes money in between. She has done it with many and the best way to influence is to lend them money to the extent, girls cannot earn it easily and in order to pay back she will let them get in this once, twice or thrice and then it becomes part of life. She also influences by giving an example of such girl who lives lavishing life, their makeup, expensive cloths by doing this. Since Zeba is so beautiful naturally she was never required make up or expensive cloths to look good, she looked stunning in her own garments she brought from Pakistan which was simple but nice.

When Shazia came to Dubai from Aligarh she had a dream to start her own business and it was important to have network which she was developing day by day. Though Zeba was Shazia's target but she knew one thing that Zeba is an innocent girl and if she forces her into this, Zeba will take extreme step such as killing herself etc.. Shazia and Zeba were coming close to each other and used to share their feelings. At one side Shazia was extremely tough to deal with but for Zeba she had a different kind of feeling and she used to tell Zeba that if she would have got Sundar she would ran away with him. Shazia never thought Zeba may take it seriously.

It is the 6th Thursday and date for Sundar and Zeba. Zeba as usual was excited and getting ready for the club but she realized that she has lost her earrings. She became disturbed and started finding it in the room but couldn't find. She was very upset as this earring was given by her mother and the only remembrance of her. Zeba knew that losing any thing made up of gold is not a good sign and that so she prays to god "Allah, please do not give any surprise to me." She went to the pub and kept waiting for Sundar; and he did not come today. She felt like she lost another valuable person in her life. She came back and cried a lot. Her face became pink and exhausted. She desperately wanted to see Sundar today but had no contact of him. This is the first time she felt that she fallen in love with Sundar but now helpless.

It is 7th Thursday; Sundar did not come again today. Zeba kept waiting for him; she couldn't find the earring as well. The feeling of missing someone is very painful; whatever we do, it feels like someone is looking at me but that person is not there. For Zeba, it was more painful as she has never spoken to Sundar and do not know anything about him, she was also not sure if he will ever come back. She was clueless about this feeling with a stranger whom she doesn't know but wanted to spend her entire life with. On the other side, her life was colorless, club used to feel dull, lights irritating and music cacophonic.

It is 7th Friday; today pub will be closed at 11.30AM because next day is dry day. Zeba is not feeling well. She doesn't want to go to pub today; she shares her feeling with Shazia. Shazia says she must come today, what if that guy also arrives. Zeba said "He won't come and I don't want him to arrive". Shazia "What if he is; and remembers if he comes, run away with him". Zeba was not interested talking about this subject and was lying down on the bed and turned her face towards the wall and covered her face by a blanket. Shazia said "OK your wish, I am going to market to bring stuff, if you need something let me know. Zeba had covered her face inside the blanket and said "nothing, I want poison and wanted to die". Shazia smiled and went outside.

The room was small with two beds both side, like a typical hostel setup. Other girls used to live in other room with sharing kitchen. Room had one mirror and a small window which was covered by an old but clean curtain; window is always closed and generally covered by curtain. After few minutes, Zeba opened her face from the curtain and said "Allah, why are you doing this with me". She had no makeup and her hair was completely messed up, face swollen like she just woke up but she was looking gorgeous. Like a fresh rose which has just blossomed. She came out of the bed and went towards the window and opened the curtain and started seeing outside. There was desert all the way long she could see, but a small tree which had green leaves, standing still in the harsh desert and surviving. She kept looking at that and a smile of hope passed on her face. She kept seeing that tree and it seems like that tree is passing hope and enthusiasm in Zeba, her face started changing from a dull to fresh. She took a long breath and then saw inside the room. She saw a shining object stuck on the corner of the pillar of the bed. First she saw at it for few seconds and suddenly jumped to see that, yes it was her earring which was lost. She started jumping as she has found the most precious thing in the world and thanks Allah for the blessing.

Shazia comes in and Zeba jumps and hugs her. Zeba "You know Shazia, I found my earring". Shazia said "That is fabulous, so are you coming today with me; you may find your man too." Zeba "No, he won't come." Shazia further says "Zeba, have hope on Allah. I am very sure he will come today. You got your luck back my darling." Shazia after some pause "And yes run away with him". Zeba didn't say anything and kept looking her earring in front of the mirror and very happy.

Zeba gets ready to go to the Pub with the hope that Sundar might come. Today pub will be closed at 11.30PM as tomorrow is holiday and liquor is not allowed to sell in the country but city will be open late because of celebration overnight. Zeba gets ready and actually positive that there may be good days. She reached and waited till 11.00PM and no sign of Sundar. She was sad but that is the life she has got so just waiting for another half an hour to go back apartment, and here you go, he is there. Mr. Sundar arrived in that place and sat on the same seat from where he used to see Zeba.

Zeba was busy looking at her palm and Shazia saw Sundar and then turns to see Zeba who was busy with her palm. She reached near Zeba and said "Did I not tell you?" and indicates her to Sundar. They saw each other and felt like running and hugging each other but there was an extreme level of happiness was there on their faces. Shazia "Remember, Run away with him". She was very happy seeing Sundar and Sundar was very happy seeing her, they were trying to control their simile but couldn't do that. They were happy and looking at each other, then same waiter comes and asks Sundar "I didn't see you for a while. You were alive." Sundar gets angry "This is how you talk to your customer?" "No Sir, if you wouldn't come today, someone would have died" and waiter looks at Zeba. Sundar and waiter both get emotional; then Sundar asks for beer. Waiter tells him that bar is closed at 11.30PM so he won't be able to finish beer; he can only offer him tea. Waiter to Sundar "Sir, tonight is amazing, you will see a different Dubai, go and see that and also takes someone with you." Waiter looks at Zeba. Sundar looks at Waiter and says "First time in your life you talked sense." Waiter says "Sir, actually I talk sense every day, but most of the people I meet lose sense after few drinks. It is but natural". Sundar stares at his face and waiter says "OK sir, enjoy".

Sundar is determined to talk to Zeba today so he takes a sip of tea and calls Zeba with 10 of 10 Dirham note. He calls her and gives her first note and asks "How are you?" Zeba says "I am fine, and you?" He gives her second note and says "I am well, thank you. What's your name?" Zeba "I am Zeba, and yours?"

Third note: Sundar "I am Sundar, you are from?" Zeba "I am from Peshawar, Pakistan, and you?"

Forth note: Sundar "I am from Kerala India, you know Kerala?" Zeba, "no, I only know India"

Fifth note: Sundar "Kerala is also called Malayalam, we are also called as Mallu" Zeba "Oh yes, I know Mallu, is that in India"

Sixth note: Sundar "yes very much, what are you doing tonight?" Zeba "Nothing much, why?"

Seventh note: Sundar "Today it is going to be an amazing night and you can see Dubai in different way" Zeba "yes, I heard that."

Eighth note: Sundar "If you don't mind can I please ask you to come with me." Zeba "I don't mind, but who will drop me home and what we will do whole night, wondering on streets?"

Ninth note: Sundar "We will chat. I will tell you about me and you tell me about yourself and we will see the city" Zeba: "Am I safe with you? Can I trust you?"

Tenth note: Sundar "very much." Zeba "OK, I will see you at 11.30PM"

Sundar: smiles and says "OK". Zeba also smiles and says "OK"

Zeba comes back with bit of preparation in nice light Pakistani suit in which the kurta is yellow, long, rounded, matching churidar salwar. She is also wearing red color scarf. The waist of Kurta has red color wide belt and beautiful sandal. Zeba was looking amazing. Sundar on other side was on blue jeans and white shirt and looking smart. They went outside; Sundar called taxi and opened the gate of taxi for Zeba and sat other side. They didn't talk to each other just smiled looking each other. Taxi dropped them to a Restaurant in Al Makhtoum where they sat outside. Weather was pleasant and lovely wind was going on. Zeba was rolling her hand in her hair looking at Sundar and smiling. Sundar was kept looking at her and smiling. Seems they are talking through eyes.

Sundar broke the silence and asked Zeba what she would like to drink. Zeba said Tea, so Sundar ordered Tea. Sundar asked as how she landed in Dubai and that also in such a place. Then Zeba told her story to Sundar. "My mother was from Hunza valley where she meets a Pathan from Peshawar. They marry each other and my mother moves to Peshawar along with my father. After six month of marriage my mother was pregnant with me but my father didn't tell my mother that he had already married another women. My mother did not like this lie of my father so she left his house while I was in her womb and moves back to Kalash Valley where she stays with her sister and delivers me. I grown up with my mother and went to Madarsa. My mother dies when I was 15 year old, when I became 19 year old my uncle (Zeba's mother's sister's husband) brings me to Dubai and leaves saying he will come back after 6 month and take me back to Pakistan."

Zeba is so innocent she believes in all this that her uncle will come and take her back. Sundar understands everything now. They started talking about Pakistan and India, their family, food etc. Sundar ordered dinner; Zeba guessed Sundar must be a vegetarian so settled down on Vegetarian food only. It was pretty late in night so Sundar took a taxi and dropped Zeba near her apartment. Sundar asked if she has seen the city, Zeba said not yet. So Sundar again asked if she is OK to see the city as tomorrow is off anyway in the Pub. She said yes she won't mind. They decided to meet again at 12PM outside Zeba's apartment.

Zeba reached her place and saw Shazia, all were excited to know what all happened. Zeba told entire story and people were shocked they just had dinner and did not talk anything about spending night together. Shazia was quite for a while and then again said – "I am right you must run away with that guy since that kind of person is very difficult to find."

Next day Sundar and Zeba at 12PM, Zeba is wearing blue color suit of the similar design she was wearing day before with orange color scarf and wide belt of same color. She used to cover her head with that scarf so she looked like a full moon reflection in the blue color ocean. They roam around the city, eats different thing and very happy together. Both have never felt such happiness ever in her entire life. It seems the best day for each other life. At the end of the day when Sundar was supposed to drop Zeba at her house, Sundar asked if she would like to have ice cream. She said yes.

Sundar and Zeba both are eating ice-cream. Sundar expressed that it is the best day of his life, Zeba expressed the same. After some pause and few bite of ice cream, Sundar said he has to leave Dubai in a week and have to go back to India. Zeba became sad and started sinking; Sundar could read her face and the pain she felt knowing this. She was trying to stop crying and focusing on eating ice cream but couldn't stop her tears coming out of her eyes. Sundar asked if she is alright. Zeba indicated by waiving her head yes. Sundar couldn't say a word and stopped eating ice cream.

Sundar took courage to say his feeling to Zeba "Zeba, I will miss you and feel like my life is empty without you. I don't know what has happened to me but it is very unique feeling I have lived in last two months. In last two month Dubai which is desert seems a green and pleasant place and all that feeling was because I waited for every Thursday to meet you. I think I love you to an extent I have no desire in my life but to live with you." Zeba: "I have no one in my family. I do not know why I came here in Dubai, as of now you are the only one I can think of close to me. So I do not know what to say but I need you to hold me in your hands and walk with me. After I met you it feels like I know you for many years." Zeba then keep looking at him and expecting Sundar to say something, Sundar further says: "I will be honest with you that I am from Tamil Brahman family and my parents will never support this relationship but I can promise you that I will love you more than anything in my life." Zeba keep looking at him. Sundar "Will you please marry me?" Zeba keep looking at him and a whisper comes in her ear "Zeba, run away with him." She says yes. Sundar is very happy. He holds her hand and kisses it. Both smiles and then sees at each other and then laugh.

Sundar asks about her Passport and tells her that he would sort out her VISA for India and will take her along. Sundar takes her passport and tells her that he will meet her in front of her apartment on coming Wednesday at 12PM. He will have her Passport, VISA and Ticket for India. She must come in a simple dress with some very basic cloth without other knowing where she is going. Zeba agrees to the plan of Sundar and then they finish ice cream and Sundar drops her to her apartment.

It is Wednesday, Zeba comes out waits for him outside his house, Sundar comes exactly at 12PM in a taxi. Zeba sits in the taxi and they proceed to the Airport, here they take a flight India.

Chapter 3: Sundar and Zeba in India

A flight lands in India and then shows Sundar and Zeba walking together holding hand of each other. They approach an immigration officer, and hand over both the passports to him. Immigration officer sees both of them and asks "Are you together?"

Sundar says "Yes sir."

Immigration officer: "Where did you meet?"

Sundar: "Sir in Dubai."

Immigration officer: "Any reason to bring her India?"

Sundar "Marriage."

Immigration Officer: "Sundar Ramachandran Iyer, marrying a girl from Pakistan?"

Sundar "yes sir, am I doing any mistake."

Immigration officer sees Zeba for few seconds and says "NO"

In India, they first reach Delhi then Ajmer where they marry in a Muslim way and then again to a Mangalore where they marry in Hindu way. Zeba now starts living with Sundar. They love each other more than anything and more than that they care for each other. They move city to city. Zeba has a unique habit of keeping bus, train, flight ticket, any bills such as electricity etc. in her safe box (given by mother). Time passes and now they are living in Jorhat Assam where Zeba is 7 month pregnant by Sundar's child.

Sundar is caring Zeba during this period and they live a very happy life.

One day Sundar asks Zeba that he is going outside to bring some household stuff in few minutes. He kisses Zeba on her forehead (which he usually does before leaving). Time pass, it is an hour, 2 hour, 5 hour then whole day and then entire night. Sundar doesn't come back. Zeba is very upset with the disappearance of Sundar and clueless as what has happened to Sundar. She has no connect with any of Sundar relative in India so that she could find him, only one person she knew in last few years is Shazia other than Sundar.

After all wait, she then searches her box and found the number of Dubai Club where she used to work; Zeba comes to a telephone booth to call Shazia. She speaks to waiter and he was kind to tell her that Shazia moved back to India and also share Shazia's number with Zeba. Zeba calls Shazia in India number and she was lucky to talk to her and tells her story briefly, Zeba also requests Shazia to come to Jorhat, Shazia agrees. Shazia reaches Jorhat where Zeba is pregnant and in a very depressed and bad situation, her health worsens every day. Shazia takes care of her very well and stays there.

Chapter 4: Zeenat arrives

A night, it was raining like cats and dogs. It seems god wanted to clean every road, street, houses, dirt, mud and whatever is on the way. As a great thing is happening and on top it is lightening like never before. Zeba started labor and shouting with a pain. In the situation outside, Shazia can't take her to hospital so she asks ladies from neighborhood to help her. 3 More ladies arrive from household and help Shazia in Zeba's delivery. After so much of pain, blood and shout, Zeba delivers a girl.

Shazia takes that girl in her hand and says – Masha Allah I have never seen such a beautiful girl in my entire life. Other ladies see Zeenat and say – An angel has arrived on earth today. Shazia wraps Zeenat in pink towel and turns to Zeba. Zeba's health is in very bad shape now; so much of blood has come from her body and because of serious stress she has almost given up. All discuss Zeba's situation and decided to consult doctor, one among those lady calls a doctor from her house. Zeba with indication calls Shazia, she indicates to open a cupboard and bring the box which is kept in the Cupboard. She calls Shazia near her and holds her hand and says in a diminishing voice – "Please take care of my daughter -Zeenat, She is yours now. When she grows up, please give her this box and ask her to find her father and ask him why has he left me and her?" Shazia says "Nothing is going to happen to you, you please rest." Zeba holds her hand tightly her eye requests for a promise from Shazia. Shazia promises "I will do whatever you have just said, but please have a faith on Allah, you will be alright."

Zeba smiles and gives an indication that she is sleeping now.

Doctor arrives and checks Zeba and informs that she is no more alive. Because of excessive blood loss and depression, she has given up. Shazia sits near Zeba and sees her face. Zeba face was glowing like a sunset beauty; she was looking as pretty as she used to look before. Shazia doesn't cry; she covers her face with the blanket. She sees baby Zeenat wrapped in pink cloth, Shazia looks at Zeenat for almost a second and very crude and cunning smile on her face.

Shazia buries Zeba's bodies and having Zeenat in her hand, few people are present along with a Maulwi Sahab who does ritual for her body. Shazia then seen at the Railway Station and waiting for the train, with a basket where Zeba's box is kept. She feeds milk to Zeenat. Train arrives at the platform, Shazia gets into the train -Tinsukia Mail which will take her to Aligarh. Train starts and goes towards JalpaiguRi, Kisanganj, Katihar, Barauni, Patna, Mugalsarai, Kanpur and then Aligarh. She comes out of the Train and blackout.

Chapter 5: ZEENAT as a Kid

After 7 years. It is 5AM in the morning; sky looks little bright and hope of light which indicates a great day is ahead. It starts with morning Azan.

It's now 6.30AM in the morning, a person wearing Kurta, Payjama and a half sweater walking fast in the narrow street of Aligarh. People in the street seems know him and greeting him saying "Assalam Valekum Shahjad Mia" and he quietly answering (walekulum assalam) as he is trying to hide his face. Shajad mia is a mid aged guy who became Maulwi at early age because his father used to be a very respected and known Maulwi of his time. After his death, he has been crowned as Maulwi. Shahjad has fewer agendums in his life, such as taking care of Masjid and earns his living by tuition. He has maintained decent rapport within the society and earned respect. The reason for him taking Tuition is to earn household as he knew it is difficult to run a family by only engaged in Masjid.

Zeenat has grown up and 7 years now, amazingly beautiful girl; she mesmerizes everyone with her witty answers and smartness. Zeenat is everyone's favorite. Shahjad sees her for first time. Though he is not a pervert guy but like a typical man he also couldn't control his wild imagination for Zeenat but felt better to control it as she is too small. From Shahjad perspective, she could achieve Zeenat only by respect and not by his action or personality.

Shazia is known as Badi Apa in Aligarh and famous for obvious reasons. Shazia has excellent connect with Police,

Politicians and Businessmen as she used to take care of them very well. She has built network in Dubai as well. She operates out of Aligarh and her target are girls from poor families in UP. She lends money to the family, package the girl and then sends them to various parts of India and abroad as per demand.

Shajad has been invited by Badi Apa for a special purpose. Shahjad was very curious to know what can be that special purpose in which Badi Apa had called him so early in the morning. Shahjad reaches Badi Apa house, gate is open but he still knocks the door with help of big lock, a sound comes from inside, "who is there?" Shajad murmurs "Badi Apa, I am Shahjad", a sound comes from inside "Oh Mia Shahjad, come in, no one knocks our door, we like to welcome people here and keep our doors open. (Badi Apa laughs). Shahjad settles in a block in front of rocking chair where Badi Apa sits. Badi Apa asks "Shahjad Mia, you will definitely like to have tea, right?" Shahjad says "Of course Badi Apa". Badi Apa comes with a plate with two cups and offers him one cup. Both take the sip of the tea. Like in a typical morning, tea vapor is coming out of the cup and they enjoy the sip.

In last seven years Badi apa has gained little weight but her beauty remains the same, as she has her own set of lovers. Shahjad also sees her with his witty eyes but an indication comes from Badi Apa is "you can't afford me." Badi apa now lives in a place which has one common living area and multiple rooms inside. Living area has a hanging chair and few cubes and a small table. Badi apa is sitting on the hanging chair and Shahjad on the Cubes. Badi apa start talking and shares her context of discussion: "Shahjad Mia, you know I have a daughter Zeenat, I am really concerned as she is growing and seven year now. I want you to take her private tuition so that she learns how to speak and behave in a higher society. If she speak well and know how to behave in higher society, she can help in my retirement (with cunning style)." Shahjad tells "Badi Apa, you also want Zeenat to do all those your other girls are doing?" Shazia "not as low like us, She is Zeenat and she will win the heart of big people and for that she must speak English and know how to talk and behave. Hope you got the perspective."

Shahjad agrees then he sees Zeenat coming near Badi Apa and hugs her and asks "Badi Apa, why do people study?" Badi Apa says "Zeenat my darling, people study so that they can become better human being." Zeenat further asks "Are we not a better human being?" Shahjad says "Zeenat my dear, please come to me, I will tell you why people study?" Badi Apa to Zeenat "My darling, meet Mia Shahjad, he is your mentor now and will answer all your question, crazy questions too." Shahjad smiles and calls Zennat near him. Zeenat takes a cube and sits in front of him.

Zeenat "Now you are my mentor, what is the difference between a mentor and a teacher?"

Shahjad says "I will teach you the subject such as math, history literature etc. and also mend to become a better human being."

Zeenat "What is a fault in me?"

Shahjad laughs and says "My dear Zeenat, with study we learn new things about ourselves and this world so that we are better aware of them and become better human being."

Zeenat "OK, now please tell me why do we study?"

Shahjad explains "Have you sees a river?"

Zeenat says "yes".

Shahjad "There are two sides of river, right?

Zeenat, "Yes Right"

Shahjad, "Well, our life is also same, we have two sides of our life like a river, one side is where we are standing right now, other side is where we have better life. Now we need to learn swimming and cross the river. Same way with studies we learn new things and become better human being"

Zeenat "Then I want to study more and more because I wanted to be the best….!"

Then she looks at Shahjad and Badi Apa, smiles and disappears for playing.

Chapter 6: Gaurav in Aligarh

Gaurav stays near Badi Apa's house and can see Badi Apa's roof from his room's window. Gaurav's father is working in a lock making factory as floor manager. Gaurav is only son of their parents so he lives in highly protected and pampered environment. His mother is over possessive about him so he is becoming adamant in most of the thing he does. When he was 11 year old he saw Zeenat on the roof of Badi Apa's house. At that age, Gaurav was totally mesmerized seeing Zeenat for the first time. He had never seen such a face and beauty like Zeenat. This curiosity made him so intrigued that in entire day he was only looking to have a glance of Zeenat and used to do every possible thing he could to get one. His mother got to know this and complained this to his father. His father also became upset and decided to take drastic to relocate to Mumbai in the same company.

But for Gaurav it wasn't easy to forget Zeenat, he wanted to speak to Zeenat before going away from Aligarh so a he decided to go to Badi Apa's house and speak to her. It was a very courageous step he did by entering the house of Badi Apa, everyone was surprised to see him and he became matter of fun and curiosity. Gaurav's only objective was to know the name of the girl he is after. While he was getting teased by other members he saw his dream girl running from one room to other and Badi Apa saying her name – "Zeenat, listen my dear". Gaurav smiled and started looking at Zeenat, while Zeenat was running from one side to other side she looked prominently at Gaurav. By the time Badi Apa approached Gaurav and grabbed him, Gaurav ran away from there. Badi Apa asked everyone – "Who was that guy?" All indicated "they don't know"

Gaurav father packs his bag and puts all in a rickshaw for the train station. Gaurav sees from his window for last time and says – Zeenat, I will find you.

Chapter 7: Zeenat with Mia Shahjad and Badi Apa

It is quite obvious that by having Zeenat, Badi Apa has got a diamond stone which has not been finished yet and Badi Apa has plan to get the maximum price out of it. Badi Apa was protective about Zeenat as per her going outside and meeting new people may spoil her mind and Apa may lose her. Same time she doesn't want to leave any wire unturned when it comes to finish the diamond. Zeenat is small and unaware of this intention of Badi Apa, for Zeenat this is the world. However, Shahjad is aware of her intention but he also has his own intention with Zeenat.

Zeenat is getting mend by Mulla Shahjad, though the age gap between them are very wide Shahjad's soft corner about Zeenat is quite obvious and as per his perspective to get respect, he tries to make sure Zeenat doesn't miss anything she could have achieved in a proper school. Zeenat takes interest in study and started enjoying every bit of it. Shahjad's assignment was to teach some basic stuff so that Zeenat knows how to behave and talk within the higher society. Zeenat on other side, getting deeper in the world of Knowledge and Wisdom. Shahjad used to tell Zeenat that the best thing that could happen in her life is the passion for learning, the day she makes knowledge her purpose to live; she will get her best friend who will stay with her together for the entire life. Zeenat actually got the best friend.

Days passed by and Zeenat is 15 years now. By this time Zeenat managed to study very well and by the help of Shahjad she also passed 10th exam with very good marks.

Till this Badi Apa was not much bothered about Zeenat and her voraciousness for learning and knowledge, but when she saw Zeenat's 10th results, she became upset and disturbed. Zeenat on other side, started to know that Badi Apa is not very keen with her studies and she has other intentions. She couldn't figure out why a mother will force her child for the act of prostitution but that was the reality and the mystery she was living with and totally unaware with the future scenarios.

Getting education for a sex worker's child is not welcomed in our society. Unfortunately school teachers also treat them differently and think that they may spoil the reputation of school. Zeenat was also facing something similar, but she was boldly managing this with her attitude and her 10th results put a full stop to everyone mouth. She also made sure that all the young girls within the sex worker society must study. Zeenat now wanted to study further and maybe from different city as in Aligarh it has become really difficult for her to stay out of the shadow of Badi Apa's business.

It was very unfortunate that sex worker also force their children to get in the same profession they are in. But Zeenat has completely changed the perspective among them and everyone was in favor of Zeenat but they did not have courage to speak and support Zeenat in front of Badi Apa. So Zeenat decided to confront Badi Apa by herself and figure out a way. The biggest hurdle for her was Shahjad and Shabnam so she found the solution for them.

Shabnam is Badi Apa's best friend and knows everything about Badi Apa and her business. So far she helps in managing Badi Apa's nexus but after Zeenat's help she also focuses on her own business of knitting. The irony is that Shabnam used to brainwash Badi Apa during Zeenat's study but now Zeenat is like angel for her who changed her life. Now she is biggest supporter that Zeenat must study further.

After Zeenat success in 10th exam, Shahjad mia's tuition demand jumped significantly though his intention still continues. Zeenat figured out this and gave a total different perspective that if he doesn't support further studies of Zeenat, the respect he has gained from people and from her will vanish within few seconds. For Shahjad the new life was more important than anything else so he became his advocate of further studies and from outside.

Zeenat is a highly confident, smart and learned girl and by now she knew the intention of Badi Apa with respect to her future so she decides to confront her and made her agree for her further studies. Zeenat sits with Badi Apa and ask her as why she doesn't want her to study further, Badi Apa gives a vague reason of her old age etc. and the big empire she has built.

Zeenat explains it politely "It is not necessary that I need to sell my flesh to take care of your old age. You have taken care of me so far and for me to reach to the height of the same field you want me to go, then you let me see the world." Zeenat further added "If I see the world and different kind of people in the world, I will know how to handle them and it will help me to take your empire to next level. Don't you want that? Or you want me to start from the place you have started and struggle whole life to reach here." Badi Apa couldn't say anything to Zeenat as she was so convincing and confident. So she decided to consult her known person in Mumbai named Rahman.

Rahman is Badi Apa's old known person who also comes from Aligarh, Rahman is working in a popular Bar in Mumbai. His job is to manage the collections every night. Rahman is the master of collection businesses and he knows how to utilize girls to maximize collection. He is a very proficient in his work but he doesn't believe in forcing girls to do anything they don't like. Rahman is a married guy but doesn't have child. He knows Badi Apa from a long time and agrees to let Zeenat stay in his house in Mumbai and complete her next level of education – 12th.

Rahman saw Zeenat's beauty and thought of utilize that to his own benefit so he sought an advice from Badi Apa to let Zeenat work in bar and help him in the collections as her math is good. Badi Apa agrees to let Zeenat help Rahman, in this way Zeenat will get exposed to total new world and new people. But Badi Apa takes promise from Rahman that he will protect her and never let any eye persuade her. Rahman promises this to Badi Apa.

Zeenat goes to school in the day time and in night she stays in Bar for 3 hours. It was very hectic schedule but that is something she has to do if she has to stay in Mumbai. To keep the secrecy, Rahman gives another name to Zeenat – Ankita.

Chapter 8 - Uttara in Dance Club

Zeenat name was changed to Ankita as it is common practice among dance bars in Mumbai. Zeenat has started spending 3 hours every day in the bar and helps in collections from other girls. To understand this entire process Zeenat was supposed to spend time in bar and stand like other girls. Initially Zeenat was uncomfortable in the place but she started gelling up with other girls and knowing their problem, that gave her enthusiasm to help these girls' live better lives.

After coming to Mumbai Zeenat used to think as what kind of mother she has got who wanted to push her in such a clumsy world. But for her surprise she found unbelievable stories of parents and relatives who have forced their own girls into this place. Zeenat started understanding the problem and one common reason she could find was lack of proper education to all these girls. Zeenat used to observe that girls are not able to count the money properly or understand some basics necessities of the world such as why insurance is required, what are the basic hygiene factors everyone must know, what kind of effect smoking can do in their lives. She started explaining this to girls and slowly girls started loving Zeenat for her knowledge and intellect. Some girls requested Zeenat to organize English and math classes for them.

Zeenat popularity started increasing day by day among girls and girls started trusting her. Initially girls were fighting with Rahman for the % of money, after Zeenat's explanation of the entire eco system and the revenue mechanism of the bar they started cooperating in this whole process. She simply used to explain how much cash is coming every day, daily expenses, staff salaries, maintenance, police commission and % share of everyone based on their contribution. It was easy for all of them to understand and start cooperating; Rahman was very happy to see Zeenat's way of simplifying the complex problem and solving it.

During this process Zeenat got to know that few girls are getting into prostitution as they needed instant money. So she started "sister fund" where all girl will donate some money and whenever required in case of urgency can be given to the needed one.

Another biggest problem she could find was girl's future. She saw that young girl makes decent money and slowly that fades away as she grows. She started a process of getting them trained for vocational course such as Beauty Parlor, Tailoring, Handmade Bags etc. so that girls find their way out of this world and get other way of living with decent earning.

Zeenat also made sure that girls started taking education seriously for their next generation so that their kids don't face same humiliation her mother faced. Zeenat also helped some of the girl getting married with their soul mate which wasn't possible as their parents used to force them not to marry, otherwise their income will be in trouble. She made sure that lousy father and brother work and make earning for family and let girls live free life.

Zeenat was loved and respected by everyone and all used to say that god has sent an angel in our life. Zeenat knew one thing that "if you have to change something you don't like then you have to be in that situation until it changes the way you like". So everyday Zeenat had a reason to go to work because she was working for the reason and the appreciation gave her enthusiasm.

Chapter 9: Ankita meets Gaurav

Gaurav on other side grew up being a rebellion personality and is unstable trying to do many things and not linking anything. His situation was like a typical spoiled child who has no direction in life; his father blames his mother for his condition. He tried to be in a band as a singer but later fought with them, then he decided to pursue job in a bank and then beats his boss as his boss was trying to molest a girl, then he tried journalism, while he was doing journalism he realized that a journalist does everything else than journalism. During his stint as so called journalist he visited Dance Bar accidently.

Gaurav and cameraman searching for cheap place to drink and got into a dance bar in Mumbai. When both of them finished two pegs police raids in Dance Bar, Gaurav seeing this started laughing so Police caught him and started asking question and took him with them. When they put him in the van, Gaurav realized he is journalist and that can help him get rid of Police. He told police that he is a Journalist and doing a research on Dance Bars. It was all false but helped Gaurav to escape from Police. He again came back in the bar to get his cameraman who was trapped inside. When he came inside Rahman advised him to stay in the bar for some time to avoid any doubt. He waited and then a fresh set of pretty girls arrive inside the bar. He saw everyone and stuck on one face Ankita, it seems he has seen that face elsewhere but not able to figure out where.

Gaurav got addicted to visit that Bar and started saying everyone that he is doing study on Dance Bars and the life of girls but the agenda was only to see Ankita. Ankita on other hand smiled seeing Gaurav and started liking him because Gaurav was not like typical crowd. Gaurav was clueless about the fact as how he knows her.

Rahman noticed everything about Gaurav and Ankita coming closer and it worried him so he decided to stop Ankita coming in bar.

<u>**Chapter 10: Gaurav's dream**</u>

Today Gaurav woke up very early to shoot a political party assembly in Shivaji Stadium, when he comes back to office in the evening he was quite tired so slept on his chair keeping his head on the table.

Gaurav is in Aligarh and walking in the street with a lolly pop in his hand and giving it to small Zeenat. Zeenat takes it and runs away, this continues and Zeenat grown up and become Ankita now. When Zeenat becomes Ankita, Badi Apa arrives and takes her inside, Gaurav couldn't do anything. He is trying to enter but couldn't. Gaurav wakes up with sweat all over his face. It was dream. Gaurav is lost between Zeenat and Ankita.

He decided to visit the Bar and enquire more about Ankita.

Gaurav reaches pub but unfortunately Ankita was not there so he enquired from a girl who was in last few weeks appeared closest to Ankita. Name of that girl was Roshani, Roshani said Ankita is not well today but she can pass the message to her. Gaurav took a tissue and wrote a brief letter for Ankita.

Ankita – I don't know why but seems I know you from ages. I wanted to meet you, know about you and tell you who I am and what I do. Can we please meet over coffee tomorrow? It will be great if you can confirm by SMS or otherwise I will wait for you between 3 to 6PM in Inorbit Mall in Malad. Only yours, Gaurav (Mobile Number). He gave that letter to Roshni and requested to give it to Ankita.

Rahman saw everything.

Second day, he did not get any call from Ankita and reaches that Pub again. He couldn't meet Roshni as well as Ankita. Gaurav became little nervous and approached Rahman. Rahman brought him outside and told him that the place he is right now is not the place to search for love. People come here to have fun and shred their cash. And the person Gaurav is serious about is something beyond his reach so better forget her or otherwise consequences may not be favorable.

Gaurav insisted and became bit aggressive to know about Ankita and her background. Rahman advices bouncers to politely through him outside. A bouncer wearing white dress (looks like Marathi politician) very politely says Gaurav to go back home and never come here again as it is not a place for him.

Gaurav on other side did not give up; he tried entering pub wearing different dresses but unfortunately every time the bouncer in white dress catches him and politely requests him to go home.

One day it is 7AM in the morning, Gaurav after completing his night schedule was going back home. It was a lovely morning and Gaurav was on his bike going slow through Worli sea face and enjoying the view. Suddenly he saw a known face standing in the south Worli Bus station, it was Roshani. Gaurav was bit ahead so stopped his bike and came back by pushing his leg. He was in front of Roshni and opened his helmet. Roshni saw him and suddenly realizes who he is and started running towards north in the pavement area. To chase her, Gaurav parked his bike and started chasing her back. Roshni ran far and then reached a dead end where she got into the sea side. Gaurav by that time was totally exhausted and asked the reason for running. Roshni started crying, and blamed herself for everything happened. Gaurav was clueless and asked Roshni to elaborate.

Roshni: that day Rahman saw you gave me a letter, he came and asked what is that? I smiled and advised him to ignore so he did knowing that letter is for me. I gave that letter to Ankita and she was ready to meet you between 3 to 6PM. She planned to watch you for some time and then meet you. I wasn't very happy seeing her so happy and getting her ready. Frankly speaking, I had never seen her so happy to meet any boy. So I got jealous and decided to inform Rahman about the meeting. When she was about to come out of her room, Rahman came and taken her away somewhere and after that I don't know where is she. They transferred me to another shady bar in Dadar which I hate but have no choice. Gaurav is hearing everything quietly and then Roshani says "by the way her name is not Ankita, it's Zeenat". Gaurav was surprised and asked again – "sorry what's her name. Roshni says "it is Zeenat not Ankita". Gaurav further says- "and she is from Aligarh". Roshani – "how do you know that?" Gaurav –"because I am supposed to know that, not only me. Even god wanted me to know that." Roshni – "That's great to know. But how will you find her now?".

Gaurav felt excited then suddenly exhausted and sat on the rock there. Gaurav – "I don't know that, but if god has brought me in this, he will bring me out of this and also show me how to find her."

Possible intermission

Chapter 11: Gaurav chase for Zeenat

Gaurav reaches bar little early and asks white dress bouncer to call Rahman. Rahman comes out and sees Gaurav and shows a surprise cum concerned face.

Rahman – "what you want now?"

Gaurav – "Can we have man to man talk?"

Rahman liked Gaurav's confidence and gets inside the pub, both drinking tea. Rahman is surprised to know that Gaurav knows Zeenat.

Gaurav tells him "I know Zeenat from very early days when I first saw her in Aligarh, this time God indicated me to be with her in her journey. It is more than unusual, either you will help me or god will help me. You decide."

Rahman – "Zeenat is a great soul, I have seen many girls coming out from disturbed to very poor background but Zeenat was not like them from beginning. She has a Midas touch in her persona, wherever she goes people just fall in love with her. Not for her beauty or the way she looks but for the approach she has for life".

Gaurav is curious now. Rahman further says – "Zeenat loves studying, I have seen that when a girl started earning, they enjoy this life and focus on earning more as Life is very short. Dance bar girl's real life is only 5 years, afterwards they move into prostitution and live pathetic life. Zeenat shown them path and arranged education and vocational courses for them so that they can transition to better job, such as Retail Shop, Beauty Saloon, Call centre etc. This is brilliant, she has changed many girls life and she is role model for everyone."

Gaurav- "where is she now?".

Rahman-"before I tell you where is she now, it is better you tell me what you want from her".

Gaurav-"I wanted to help her in her journey".

Rahman- (smiles) she is Zeenat, she is god's angel who has come on this earth to change lives; she doesn't need you to help her. You however can learn her if you are so keen."

Gaurav – "Yes…. yes I wanted to learn her".

Rahman – "Well, in that case you should not be sitting here but to be in Aligarh as she has completed her 12th and I had to send her back to Aligarh as per my promise to Badi Apa."

Chapter 12: Gaurav in Aligarh

Gaurav has got the purpose of life "To Learn Zeenat" and reaches Aligarh in the Badi Apa place, where he doesn't find Badi Apa nor Zeenat. The door he used to remember is closed by a big Lock, he is clueless and lost now and sat on the stairs of street and suddenly hears Azan. He suddenly get a clue and ran towards the Masjid from where he heard Azan, he asks few people and reaches to Masjid where he sees Mulla Shahjad talking to few people. He approaches Mulla and requests him to talk something important. Mulla asks the purpose and Gaurav says – "it's about Zeenat." Mulla says everyone to go back and agrees to spend time with Gaurav.

Mull and Gaurav reaches to a place where Mulla opens a lock and gets inside. Both Mull and Gaurav are drinking Tea, Mulla: "Zeenat is a god's gift to mankind. I remember when Zeenat was 7 year old and I got an assignment to teach her some basic know how and little bit of English. When I met her once she asked me the reason of study. I told her that studies lighten not only our life but also others life. She actually understood and also applied it in her life." Mulla continues: - "I know how she motivated other member of Apa's so called family to send their children to school and get educated. Apa was not in favor of that but she couldn't stop anyone to go to school when she loses an argument with Zeenat about her poor skills of math."

Mulla continues – "I made sure, Zeenat learns every aspect of a proper education and the best part was Zeenat not only applied it in her day to day life she continuously learn from her surroundings and tries to make it better world to be in. She also changed my life in the meanwhile.

Mulla – A famous saint says "To acquire knowledge, one must study; but to acquire wisdom, one must observe." I have not seen anyone as observant as Zeenat. She in fact gets to know what Apa wanted from her at the age of 10 and also realized that the only way to come out of this clumsy place is study hard and that is what she did."

Gaurav told Mulla that he saw Zeenat in Mumbai where she completed her 12th. After that he heard that she is in Aligarh. Mulla did not have any clue about Zeenat's return so they decided to meet Badi Apa's friend Shabana.

They have a tea in Shabnam's house and Shabanam shares that she was living in hell with Badi Apa, Zeenat observed that Shabnam has an amazing knitting skills so she helped her start her own business of Knitting and today she has 5 staff working for her and she is living a respectful life. Since she is closed to Badi Apa she knew that Badi Apa was upset with Zeenat's study and her interest in study, so she decided to take her to Hyderabad and SELL her to a Sheikh. Shabanam wanted to help Zeenat but unfortunately she is very scared from Badi Apa and couldn't do anything.

Shabnam also mentioned "I know one thing for sure that God has send Zeenat to change lives, and her journey are touching many lives so it may be Allah marzi to let Zeenat go to Hyderabad."

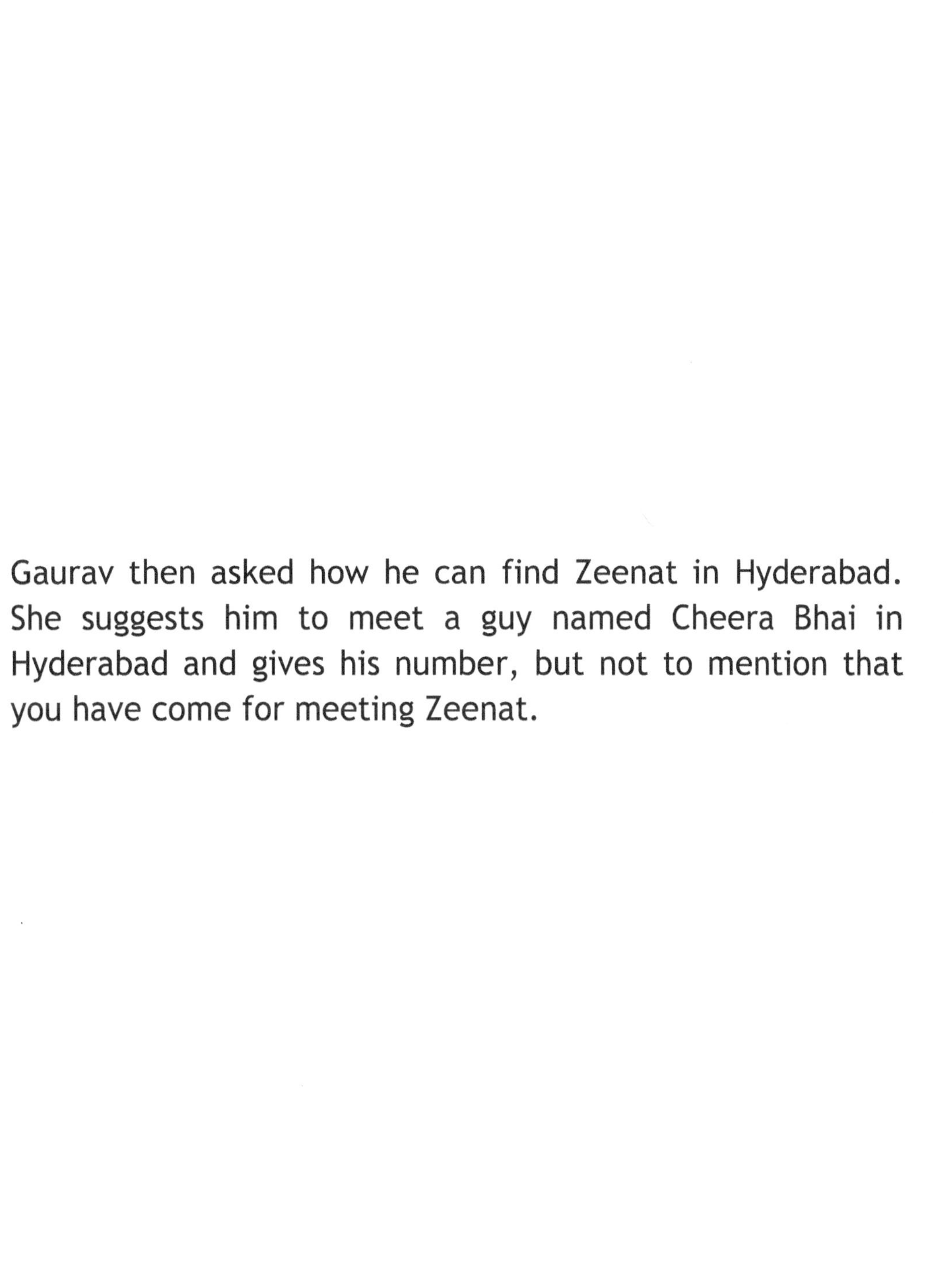

Gaurav then asked how he can find Zeenat in Hyderabad. She suggests him to meet a guy named Cheera Bhai in Hyderabad and gives his number, but not to mention that you have come for meeting Zeenat.

Chapter 13: Gaurav in Hyderabad

Gaurav travels to Hyderabad along with his cameraman named Sanu and contacts Cheera Bhai. Cheera Bhai is Badi Apa's left hand and manages business of selling girls to Sheikh from Middle East. It is a big nexus; it was difficult for Gaurva to crack this whole thing so he decided to play a game. He meets Cheera and creates a story that he has a Sheikh friend from Middle East who is keen to buy a young girl and Cheera must arrange them in a hotel room. He convinces his cameraman to act like sheikh, Sanu was nervous but for Gaurav and curiosity of seeing so many girls he agrees to do so.

Gaurav arranges this thinking he will meet Zeenat but unfortunately he couldn't meet Zeenat in this trap. But he recorded everything very smartly. He later meets Cheera and tells him to arrange someone very special, Cheera pretend not to understand that, so Gaurav indicates the one who has come from Aligarh. Cheera is surprised and threatens to kill Gaurav. Gaurav politely tells him to chill as he has recorded his every act and he can show it to police and all Cheera's business will be devastated. Gaurav also shows him his Journalist card so that Cheera is in total control.

Cheera then shares what has happened between Zeenat and Badi Apa in Hyderabad which Cheera arranged and saw everything. Cheera tells the story:

After Zeenat's return to Aligarh, Badi Apa instructed Cheera to arrange a big bang show to sell Zeenat of the price never happened before. Cheera arranges a close function where Sheikh came from different part of Middle East countries to buy a Girl. The name and identity of the girl was kept secret but has been promoted as they are going to part of most amazing auction of their lives.

Everything was arranged to the perfection, Zeenat has been prepared the best way and she was looking stunning in long red color dress with most expensive Jewelries. Zeenat knew that she is in full trap but she wanted to experience this and understand what actually happens.

And the function starts with a dance, and after that Badi Apa enters the place and starts the function- "Now I present a beauty of the world; A diamond which has been kept under the wrap for 17 years; A breed no one could imagine" everyone was curious like never before.

Badi Apa continues – "A breed between A Brahmin boy from a place in Kerala named Palakkad and a girl from Hunza Valley, Pakistan - ZEENAT, the beauty of the god." Zeenat was in a very unique dress hearing all this and totally shocked. And the auction starts. Finally Zeenat is sold and a sheikh from Saudi Arabia has purchased her who lives in Dubai. Then come the same song which was running before and three guys stands from three directions and showers the money on Zeenat.

Zeenat, after this drama is sitting in a room with extreme anger and eyes full of tears. Badi Apa comes with a box wrapped with a nice cloth and sits near her and holds her hand. "Zeenat my darling, today you have created history in our world and now Badi Apa can take rest for her entire life." Zeenat doesn't speak a word. Badi Apa continues – "I know you have many questions about who you are and why did I not tell you the truth till now. I must tell you even I don't know how you came in my life and I thank god that she sent you in my life. The only thing I know is your mother name is Zeba whom I met in Dubai many years back where I used to do Mujra. Your mother was innocent and pure like rain water. She met a Tamil Brahmin named Sundar in Dubai and ran away with him. I do not know what has happened after that but she called me from Jorhat, Assam where you were born and your mother died after giving birth to you."

Badi Apa continues: "Your father left her when she was 7 months pregnant and has no clue about him after that. This is the box she gave me and told me to give it to you. Since you are going Dubai, and will live like queen, I wanted to hand over this box to you as the last sign of your mother."

Badi Apa stands as she has finished her conversation with Zeenat; then turns back "One more thing, your mother wanted you to search for your father and ask him why has he left your mother in that condition." (Cheera saw all this)

Gaurav is totally emotional hearing this story and his eyes are full of tears and anger. He sees Cheera and asks where is Zeenat? Cheera says he can't disclose that. Gaurav sees him for few seconds and starts beating him. Cheera after good dose says, Dubai.

Chapter 14: Zeenat in Dubai meets Adilah

Zeenat doesn't speak a word and gets in a flight to Dubai. She is wearing a black burka with head covered and looking like an Arabian beauty. She reaches Dubai in an apartment which looks very stylish. She sits in the couch and there is a glass table with a flower pot with orchid flower in it. Zeenat sees that flower and smells that. Then again sits on couch and keep watching flower pot and remembers the word of Badi Apa, in fact every word. "Your mother wanted you to search for your father and ask him why he has left your mother in that condition."

After sometimes a lady enters, her name is Adilah. She also wearing her black head covered dress. She comes in the room and changes the dress and comes in a nice black mini dress and lights a cigarette.

She after few puffs asks Zeenat her name.

Adilah – "What's your name baby?"

Zeenat – "sorry".

Adilah – "Is this your name – Sorry".

Zeenat – "No, Zeenat"

Adilah - "Oh such a beautiful name as like you, why did you come here. Or rather how did you come here?"

Zeenat drinks a glass of water of the table and says the story briefly with full of innocence - "I wanted to study but my so called mother who runs brothel in India wanted to sell me. In my entire life I was thinking she was my mother but I yesterday got to know that my mother is from Pakistan and my father is Tamil Brahmin. They left me in hands of Badi Apa and she sold me to you."

Adilah gets little sentimental – "not to me my dear, leave that part as you would never understand this whole dynamics." Zeenat started crying and sees the box.

Adilah ask "what is this?"

Zeenat innocently says – "My mother has left this box and wanted me to find my father who left my mother before I was born. I wanted to search my father and ask why he left my mother in such a condition. And you know they first met in Dubai."

Adilah eyes had water, she lights another cigarette and says – "well, I have never done anything right but this time I will do that. I will help you find your father and I am sure I could help you get the first source from Dubai."

Adilah hugs Zeenat tightly and tells her "you relax darling and I will meet you tomorrow. If you need something you can call a guy Zunaid and he will bring it for you." After Adilah leaves Zeenat opens the box and then calls Zunaid, she gives a list to Zunaid such as large paper sheet, marker, paste it, pencil etc.

Next day, Zeenat is wearing a very nice pink dress and waiting for Adilah, Adilah comes and sees Zeenat looking so beautiful, she hugs Zeenat as she was looking so beautiful. She also saw that Zeenat has prepared a full tracking in a chart along with dates and supporting slip / document.

Adilah is very impressed and asks few questions about the track and tells Zeenat to get ready and come with her.

Zunaid drives them to Bur Dubai and reaches the same Pub where Shazia and Zeba used to work. They get to know that still there are number of girls come from Peshawar city in Pakistan to Dubai to earn money and go back. In one go they can only stay for 30 to 90 days so they maintain regular flow, Girl brings girl and they are free only when they bring replacement Girl. Zunaid who is also from Peshawar knows this and explains why Peshawar,

Zunaid: "Peshawar is located in the north west of Pakistan which is close to Afghanistan border. This area is semi rid, hilly and deserted land, this area is not as developed as Karachi or Lahore so people have to travel to many places for running their household. The maximum taxi driver comes from Peshawar so these girls. The girls look beautiful and have good demand in Dubai, it is sad but the reality."

Zeenat, Adilah and Zunaid, they all travel many parts of Dubai, see the nice places and also eats amazing food. They both cared Zeenat. Zunaid on other hand had crush on Adilah which Zeenat observes that. Zeenat figures out this and help them come together. Both Adilah and Zunaid thanks Zeenat for finding their soul mate.

One day Adilah comes and tells Zeenat that "These Shiekh has tremendous amount of money so she does not need to worry. They sometime don't even know whom they have bought, so I will replace you with other girl and you will come along with me to Pakistan where we will go with you and find your maternal side. Here is your passport with Pakistan VISA in it, Zunaid will come along with us as he knows Pakistan in and out"

Chapter 15: Zeenat, Adilah and Zunaid

Adilah, Zunaid and Zeenat travel to Pakistan and reaches Peshawar district of Pakistan, they go to Zunaid's house and Zunaid introduces Adilah as her bride and everyone is very happy. Where they marry together and Zeenat is part of every function and enjoys it fully.

After marriage, Zunaid, Adilah and Zeenat take a tour via Bus and Taxi to Hunja Valley and then Kalash valley. Here Zeenat meets her mother's family and everyone is so happy to see her. She also meets the guy who has left her mother to Dubai. He cries and pleads for guilty. Zeenat hugs him and says "If you would not have done that I would not have come here in this earth. Thank you for your action but please make sure you don't do it again with anyone else." She also takes promise from him that he will volunteer girl's education in Pakistan."

She also sees some of the photograph of her mother and gets emotional.

Zeenat changes their life too by bringing fresh energy, enthusiasm and a promise for better world.

All three come back to Peshawar now and now Zeenat is supposed to travel to India. Unfortunately Zeenat doesn't know anyone who could help her in India. So Adilah explains him "I am going to introduce you to a politician in India, He belongs to a very reputed family and he has been forced to join politics which he hates. He has lost everything during last election and took a long break. He is back to India where we will be crowned as next successor.

He needed a companion so I thought I will introduce you to him. The other fact is if people see you with him, no one in this whole world dare to touch you.”

Zeenat could understand the intention of Adilah, but by this time she is more confident that she is not scared with anything comes her way so she agrees to Adilah's plan.

Chapter 16: Zeenat is Delhi

Zeenat reaches Delhi in a very stylish Grey Jeans and a white top and to her surprise she sees a big team is waiting for her with a name card. She has been escorted like someone very special has come to India. She comes out from Airport and sits in a luxurious car. She reaches a party house where there is big rush. She has been taken to a different location where she has been advised to take rest. Zeenat there sees posters of great Indian politicians and there was small synopsis written about each one.

Then comes a young super hyper guy in white Kurta, Payjama and Bandi and greets Zeenat. "Hi, my name is Viral and I am vice president of India's largest party." Zeenat laughs shook hands with him and say "I am Zeenat and I am no one. Just a citizen of India"

Viral – "then you are very important person form me as I work for the citizen of India only."

Zeenat – "That's great. But what work did you do so far for the citizen of India"

Viral gets confused, pretend to think and then answers – "I made infrastructure such as road"

Zeenat – "That a construction company did…!"

Viral – "I helped in providing basic necessities such as water, electricity etc."

Zeenat – "That is done by nature and then utility companies. My question is what did you specifically did to make sure the citizen of India is living a better life"

Viral (long breath and pause) – he looks at Zeenat face for sometime "It is actually a deep question and no one has ever asked me this. That's why people do not relate to me as I have not done anything for them."

Zeenat – "Probably yes. Then what is next plan? You are going to be the president of India's most prestigious party tomorrow. What is in for the citizen of India by you being a national leader?"

Viral – "I am impressed by you and same time clueless. Could you please help me out further in this."

Zeenat – "Well, what you think India's biggest problem is?"

Viral – "Poverty"

Zeenat – "Good answer, but why poverty prevails?"

Viral – "Because of lack of Education"

Zeenat – "You nailed it, it is the Lack of Education. Now what are you and your party is doing to get people educated?"

Viral – "Actually nothing"

Zeenat – "Then in that case, why don't you take this matter and help India gets educated and then people of India will crown you as Prime Minister than your own people crowing you as president of your own party"

Viral – "You are right. You actually helped me to really solve my problem. Thank you so very much for this; I am your fan now. Why don't you work with me?"

Zeenat – "No, I have to study properly to make sure I deserve the post I am offered."

Viarl – "Well, that makes more sense. Thanks so much again, I am so happy to meet you."

Zeenat – "Most welcome Viral Jee and I wish you all the very best."

Zeenat – "BTW, I like your dress, do you wear this dress all the time."

Viral – "I hate this dress, but I have worn it as it party's protocol"

Zeenat – "Is this dress making you more effective to perform your duties?"

Viral – "Not exactly….!"

Zeenat – "Then why to wear it?"

Viral gets it and gives thumps up and shook hand with Zeenat and leaves.

Zeenat – "And one more thing Viral Jee, there may be more capable person in your team to be president right now. It is important for us to deserve first then desire"

Viral – smiles and says "Yes Madame."

Zeenat – "Wish you all the best"

Viral turns and says – "Please join me in party function"

In next scene, it is party's function and everyone is waiting for Viral. He comes with his young party workers along with Zeenat. Viral is wearing blue jeans, yellow T-shirt and sports shoes. All murmurs.

Viral on the stage with mike - "I met an Angel today who asked me two basic question 1) what did I do to deserve this position which you all are so desperate to give me? And my answer was -None. (Pause) And second question was what is the biggest problem of India and I am proud that I could answer that – it is lack of Basic Education."

Viral further – "I wanted to announce today that I am not taking up the position you are giving me and I recommend you to nominate the most experienced and the deserved candidate. Also, I with my team standing there (indicates a young brigade) am all set to make India better place by educating kids and people. I am going to start a campaign where all young people of India will devote his time to educate people."

Viral summarizes: "Thank you so much for all your love and I request you to please figure out what special thing you did for the citizen of India to make sure you are loved by them. So far it is NONE so please go and figure out and stop all this hailing and all. Thank you and god bless."

Gaurav is in the same event capturing the news and he sees Zeenat standing in the crowd with other members of Viral's team. Gaurav chases to reach Zeenat but he is not able to reach her. After Viral finishes his speech, he goes inside the party office and speaks separately with Zeenat and thanks her for her contribution in his life. Viral wanted Zeenat to join him in his journey but Zeenat informs him that she has more important journey of her life which she must go for.

Gaurav by that time figured out to reach Zeenat and hears her conversation with Viral.

Chapter 18: Zeenat in Ajmer and Mangalore

As soon as Zeenat comes out of Viral's party house, she sees Gaurav waiting for her and says "Your driver is waiting for you, Madame". Zeenat is very happy to see Gaurav and gets in his Jeep and they are on their way to Ajmer via beautiful Delhi - Jaipur Road.

Ajmer is where Zeba and Sundar got married in Muslim way. Zeenat remembers her mother everywhere she goes in Ajmer Sharif, she tastes every food her mother has tasted and also places she has visited. Zeenat gets emotional and travels across Ajmer Sharif and feels the warmth of her mother.

After Ajmer, Zeenat reaches train station to catch Maru Sagar Express where she thanks Gaurav to be with him and explains him that it is her journey and she must go alone and request him to focus on his work. Gaurav agrees and takes promise that she will contact him, she promises and train moves towards Mangalore, where Zeba and Sundar had married in Hindu rituals. The train goes via Jaipur, Kota, Vododara, Panvel, Madgaon and then Mangalore. She enjoys the three day journey in this train and observes the culture in completely her own way. The way dresses change from Rajasthan to Gujarat to Maharashtra to Karnataka and the food preferences as well, the way people speak different languages. But she also observed the commonality and unity when it comes to cricket and films and the fan following for Sachin Tendulkar and Shah Rukh Khan. She realizes that cricket and films are integral part of our lives and that actually helps us be together. She is truly mesmerized to see the beauty of India and the unity in diversity.

While Zeenat is enjoying her journey, she couldn't escape the prostitution nexus on her way from Ajmer to Mangalore. She meets a totally unusual short man who dresses like Pathan but talks like a Sardar, his name is Suja Logo. He works in the train pantry and sells the food and beverages. Suja Logo is a multi tasking personality; he can work from both of his hands and can do two parallel but different job. From one hand he can make omelet and from second hand Parantha. No one could guess that such a talented guy is mastermind of the prostitution and drug nexus in Goa. He picks up set of girls from Rajasthan, Gujarat and Maharashtra and supplies drugs via these girls who also involves in prostitution.

Suja Logo sees Zeenat and tries to become frank with her. When Zeenat asks about her unique name – he profoundly accepts that his name is Hindi name because people beat him black and blue whenever he is caught, that's why people call him Suja Logo (Suja - Swell up Logo - people). She could figure out that he is involved in something wrong. She started observing him by requesting him to learn his tricks of making food. Then slowly started knowing what he does. He used to meet 20 different girls in different bogies, gives some packet and whispers something in their ear. By the time Zeenat could figure out what he talks, he vanishes. In nutshell a gang of girls are going somewhere with a purpose and sort of trapped in train.

When it was night and train was going in full speed, Zeenat approached girls and asks her relation with Suja Logo but no one tells her anything. All girls thought she is also part of this gang. But Zeenat decided to track this whole thing and know the purpose.

In the morning train stops in Madgaon station and all girls get out of train and follow one direction which is led by Suja Logo. All of them get in a bus and that bus starts going towards the lake of Goa. Zeenat also gets down and smartly gets in the top of the bus and hides at the roof of it.

Bus reaches a secluded place near a lake where it seems some late night party is organized and few tents are made. She goes along with girl by hiding her face and reaches a camp. Suja Logo counts the girl and asks for their name, interestingly all say actors name with some amount such as Amir Khan 400 Crore, Salman Khan 250 Crore, Shah Rukh Khan 200 Crore. She then got to know that all girls from different cities have come to join rave party and sell drugs there. Name is their code and amount is number of unit they are carrying to sell that day. Zeenat couldn't imagine what she was seeing that day and hide herself in Suja Logo camp itself.

During day time Suja Logo tries multiple dresses so that he can look like a king for the party. He somehow sees Zeenat trying to hide her in his camp so approaches her and talks very politely "So you are here…! No problem my darling. You are so lucky you are going to see a complete new world. The different world within the world we live. So no fear and it is all about love my dear." Zeenat is hardly scared and says "Oh yes, I am looking forward to see your world". Suja says "wonderful, I knew you are smart girl. Will you be my girl today?" Zeenat sees his size, keeps her hand on his shoulder and says "Look Suja Logo, may be intentionally of by mistake I came here as I am going to south part of India for a completely different purpose. I can't tell you my purpose but it is something very important for me. Also wanted to let you know that, my people are chasing me everywhere so if they track me here, you will be in big trouble. Suja Logo says "seems like Chennai Express"

Zeenat says – "smart boy, so if you want your safety, please arrange me to go back to city or otherwise we all are in trouble." Suja agrees to it and arranges a bike for her to go to the city.

When Zeenat reaches city, she calls Gaurav and asks him if he is keen to get some really exciting cover, then take a next flight to Goa and come over Lakeside. She also takes promise that Girls should not get hurt as they are really poor and they are doing it for money. She then gets into a bus which is going to Mangalore.

She reaches Mangalore and then visits different temple in Mangalore and also goes to a place called Mudabidri which her mother has also gone, Mudabidri is famous for various worship places such as Jain and Hindu temples, Churches, Mosques and Gurudwara. A unique place in itself where all the religion are well respected and everyone lives in peace.

She remembers her mother all the way in all these places and completely in love with India and its cultural richness.

On the other side Gaurav tracks the rave party and help police crack this event. Police captures Suja Logo who was wearing dress like Shah Rukh Khan of Chennai Express.

Chapter 19: Zeenat towards Palakkad

Zeenat is now aware that his father is from Palakkad village so she decides to reach Palakkad and find his father. When she reaches there she asks for Sundar Iyer, interestingly all show her one direction, she finally reaches there and sees a big house where all members wearing white dress. She gets in the house and enquires about Sundar Iyer. It creates a chaos in that house and all talking in Tamil as who is this girl and what has she come here for.

Dadda comes out and asks her who is she. She says "my name is Zeenat and I am looking for Mr. Sundar Iyer. That old man asks "why?" Then Zeenat says "because he is my father" … big shout and chaos happens. This old guy then shouts lauder and tells everyone to keep quite.

Dadda then asks – "How can you say that Sundar Iyer is your father, she shows proof as the map. Dadda sees everything in the map and looks at Zeenat and says – "I am Dadda, your grandfather and hugs her. Everyone is emotional in the house. She takes Zeenat inside and does a great celebration. Dadda shows an Album to Zeenat which is his father's Album.

Dada says – "your father has kept this album here in my custody." He said, one day my daughter will certainly come here then show her this and say that I am her culprit and please come to me." Zeenat first time sees her father and mother picture. And whole story repeats in front of her.

Dadda says "today you couldn't meet your father is all my because of me and I am alive till today is to only meet you and apologize to you for what you have gone through. Then Dadda says entire story to Zeenat:

When Sundar called and told me that he wanted to marry your mother, I was very upset from him as he wanted to marry a Muslim Pakistani girl. I was tough and told him I would never accept her in my family and she is not welcomed here. He tried to convince me many time but I was totally adamant. He used to call and talk to me, he after sometime told me that his love is more for your mother than me. I never expected this from him so I created a plot, when he called me after long time, other member of family told him that I am on death bed and if he wants, he can come here and see me before I die.

He loved me so much that he left your mother in that crucial situation to come and meet me. When he came we have sort of captured him here for a month. He left after that and came back with full of anger, he cried and told me that he has lost his wife and his child in last one more. He doesn't even know where is his child and I am responsible for all this and left house to search for you.

He couldn't find you in any place and then left everything he was doing. What I know that he started teaching small kids which could get education as he thought god will give little mercy to him so that he will get you educated and you will find him one day. God was great and sent you here. I do not know where is he now and how could you meet him, but I know that he is punishing himself every day for the decision he has taken to leave your mother and come to meet me and I am punished everyday not to see him and you."

Dadda started crying in an apologetic posture on his knees and says sorry to Zeenat. She hugs him and promises to bring his father back.

Zeenat spends time with her Dadda and entire family and enjoying her south Indian dress, song, food etc. and thinking where her father could be. One day she opens the map and the only place left was Jorhat so she got an intuition and decided to go to Jorhat. She takes the blessing of Dadda and tells him that she knows where her father is and will bring him home.

An indication shows in map that Zeenat starts from Palakkad and reaches Jorhat.

Chapter 20: Zeenat in Jorhat

She then reaches Jorhat, and as per her intuition she sees her father there teaching small kids. She lives there for few days to watch his father teaching and caring small girls and boys from various parts of cities who couldn't afford to go to school. After watching him for few days she decides to meet him.

She meets Sundar and expresses that "I have heard about you that you are doing great job for the kids by teaching them. My name is Ankita and I am keen to help you in this endeavor. If you don't mind can I help you in this?" Sundar agrees. Time passes and Sundar keep watching her playing with the kids and it seems she look like someone of her own. Sundar remembers how Zeba used to play with kids and Ankita looks same.

Sundar started liking Ankita and started taking care of her small things. Exactly like Zeba during her sleep, Ankita's leg also comes out from blanket so Sundar covers it properly. Every action of Ankita resembles with Zeba. Sundar in his wild dream couldn't imagine that she is her own daughter.

It is almost one month now and they drink tea every morning and the way Zeba used to eat biscuit with tea, Ankita does same thing. Sundar and Ankita develop a very special bond with each other.

A day comes when they are having tea and Sundar keep staring at her.

Ankita sees Sundar, smiles and asks "What?"

Sundar says, "You know my daughter would be of the same age as yours."

Zeenat then intensely sees him in his eyes and says "how are you so sure that you have daughter as you left your wife before delivery."

Sundar is stunned hearing this and couldn't speak a word. He freezes for almost a minutes; only his eyes were filled water. He started crying and Zeenat also started crying sees him. No words are getting exchanged among themselves for almost a minute.

Zeenat then asks "Why you did not inform my mother that your father is on death bed and it is important for you to go and see him." "Why?"

Sundar cries like a baby.

He holds her hand in apologetic position to say her sorry. Zeenat hugs Sundar.

Zeenat "Please answer me why did you leave my mother and me in such a situation?"

Sundar after sometime wipes his tears and says: "I used to call my father and tried convincing him for my marriage, though he was not agreeing but I knew that the news of your birth will melt him. But that day was a black day, I called him and a family member told me that he is on death bed and if I wanted to see him I must come soon."

Sundar continues "Same time, I saw the last train of the day is going towards Jalpaigudi and then Kolkata, I was in midst of my mind and train starts. I couldn't call Zeba as I had no time and got into the train. I was so upset with my father health I did not realize that I won't get the telephone booth anywhere on the way."

He starts crying and says "I am punishing myself for my foolishness every day and teaching small kids here so that god is kind and care for you."

Zeenat keep watching him and again hugs him. Sundar is crying like a baby.

After few seconds pause, Zeenat says – "I have promised Dadda that I will bring you back home." Sundar looks at him with red eyes and indicates as how big his daughter becomes now.

They go to Palakkad.

Final chapter: Zeenat's in Palakkad

After one year:

Zeenat is in pure Tamil dress and all are preparing for her first year of home return and birthday celebration. Then Dadda suddenly falls sick and Zeenat brings her first aid box to take his blood pressure and gives him injection. Dadda is alright now and say, I would never die as my granddaughter is going to become a doctor. She is studying Medical now.

Gaurav, Shahjad, Rahman, Adilah, Zunaid and Viral are also attending the celebration which is in full swing and a shout comes from outside "ZEENAT".

Zeenat comes out and sees Badi Apa and Chira. They have come here with a little force to take her back. Badi Apa says – "Zeenat, enough now come with me." Then reaches Sundar Iyer and he asks angrily "what are you doing here."

Badi Apa indicates Chira to go and take her back, he has a gun in his hand with few goons with him and forcibly comes to hold hand of Zeenat. Gaurav tries to protect Zeenat and starts beating Chira "You never had enough in Hyderabad?" Goons started fighting with Gaurav.

Then a very unique roar sound comes from inside and everyone gives a way to Dadda to come outside. He has an old but amazingly powerful rifle and he fires twice in the air. All goon disappeared saying "DADDA….?"

Badi Apa and Chira are confused to see that.

Dadda reaches near Badi Apa, hug her and politely says "Thank you very much for taking care of my granddaughter, you are special guest today as we are celebrating her birthday and one year of home return. Please join us in this celebration." Badi Apa was surprised first and then sees the face of Dadda, she smiles.

Chira throws his gun too.

And all comes inside the house with a smile.

The End